ABC Endangered Animal Rhymes

**Written By: GaGa
(AKA) Janice Abernethy**

**Artwork By: GaGa:
(AKA) Janice Abernethy**

Copyrighted Material

Copyright © 2025 Janice Abernethy

Illustrations © 2025 Janice Abernethy

Published by Janice Abernethy

Visit My Website: jabernethy.com

E-mail: janabernethy@gmail.com

ISBN: 979-8-9933573-4-8

6 X 9 Paperback

No portion of this book may be reproduced, stored in a retrieval system, or transmitted in any form or by any means, mechanical, electronic, photocopying, recording, or otherwise, without the written permission of the publisher.

Copyrighted Material

ABC ENDANGERED ANIMAL RHYMES

Dedicated to my grandchildren, Ike and Penny. May they continue to save and enjoy the animals!.

GaGa

A is for AXOLOTL

A is for Axolotl. Mexico's my home.
Amphibians with a sizable genome.

I can regrow my limbs. I love it, don't you?
You should study our genomes so you can too.

We exist in the wild in only one place.
Critically endangered. To save us is a race.

What else can I tell you? There is so much more!
Bengal Tigers are waiting. They're next on the tour.

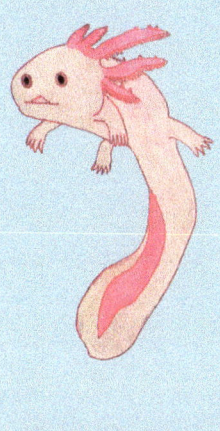

Axolotls in the wild only exist in two freshwater lakes: Lake Xochimilco and Lake Chalco.

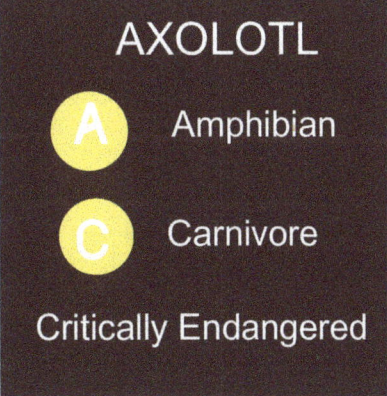

B is for
BENGAL TIGER

B is for Bengal Tiger, the most common type.
I'm endangered and special, and that's not just hype.

I stalk prey which is always, some kind of meat,
Like Buffalo, deer and wild pig for a treat.

I'm mostly in India, or China they claim.
On my coat I have stripes, no two tigers the same.

What else can I tell you? There is so much more!
But Cheetahs are waiting. They're next on the tour.

Bengal Tigers
IN THE WILD
- Bhutan
- Nepal
- China
- Bangladesh

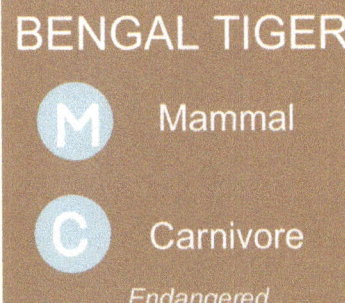

BENGAL TIGER

M — Mammal
C — Carnivore

Endangered

C is for CHEETAH

C is for Cheetah, the fastest mammal on earth.
I am proud, beautiful and I know my worth.

Once owned by warriors such as Genghis Kahn,
Trained and tamed by royalty, those times are gone.

I don't make a good pet. I require lots of space,
Expensive vet care, and live animals to chase.

What else can I tell you? There is so much more!
But Dugongs are waiting. They're next on the tour.

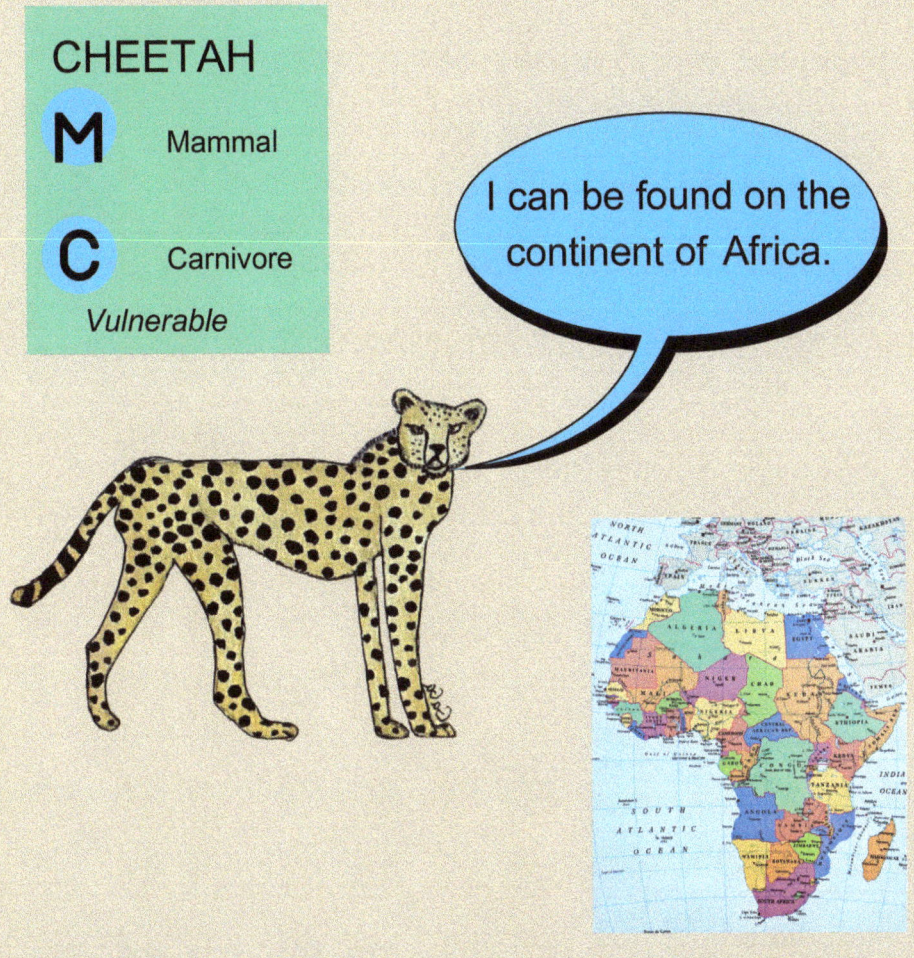

D is for
DUGONG

D is for Dugong. Cousin of the manatee.
I look like a potato, but cute as can be.

I'm a mammal that migrates on the sea floor
Munching on sea grass, until there's no more.

My population has drastically declined
Most problems I have are caused by mankind

What else can I tell you? There is so much more!
But Elephants are waiting. They're next on the tour.

I live in the warm coastal waters of the Indian Ocean and the Pacific Ocean.

DUGONG

M Mammal

H Herbivore

Critically Endangered

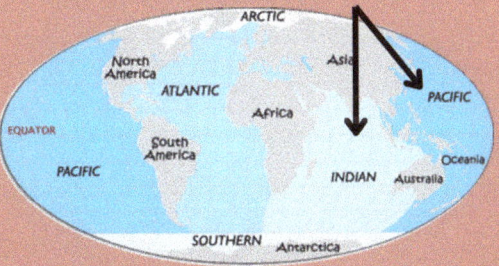

E is for
ELEPHANT

E is for Elephant—an awesome creature.
My huge brain is my most valuable feature.

My ears are like fans. They cool me off with a breeze.
And my trunk? It can hug, smell, even grab--with ease

I show feelings. I cry, play, and sometimes mourn.
And I trumpet with joy when a baby is born!

What else can I tell you? There is so much more!
But ferrets are waiting. They're next on the tour.

ELEPHANT

M Mammal

H Herbivore

Endangered

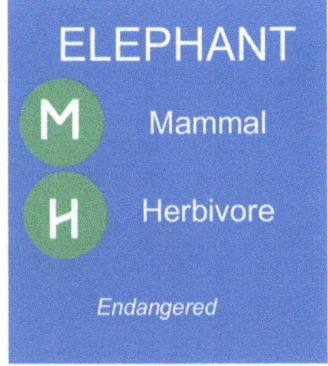

2 TYPES OF ELEPHANTS
African and Asian

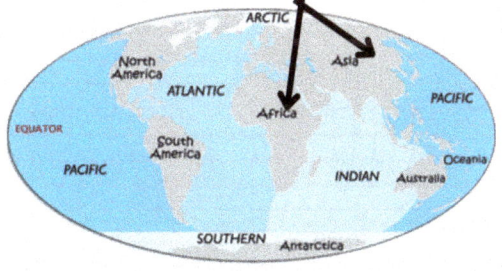

F is for
FERRET

F is for ferret. The wild black-footed ferret!
They say I'm endangered and we must repair it.

In prairie dog burrows, my mamma raised her brood,
And prairie dogs are 90% of my food.

Farmers poisoned prairie dogs and that hurt me.
Diseases, traps, bobcats, all my enemy.

What else can I tell you? There is so much more!
But giraffes are waiting. They're next on the tour.

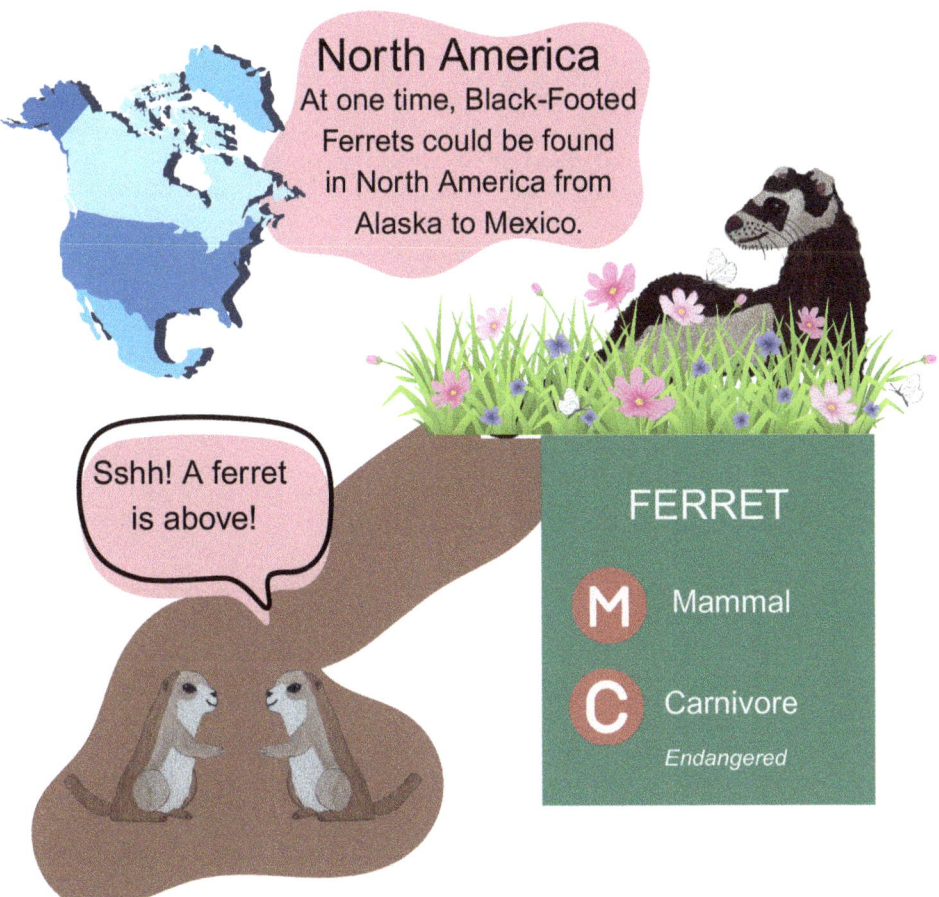

G is for GIRAFFE

G is for Giraffe. Nine subspecies of me.
Different patterns and shapes. All very trendy.

I can go without water longer than a camel.
And at 20 feet high, I'm the tallest mammal.

I splay my legs to drink because I'm built so tall.
When I fight, I use my neck like a wrecking ball.

What else can I tell you? There is so much more!
Humboldt Penguins are waiting. They're next on the tour.

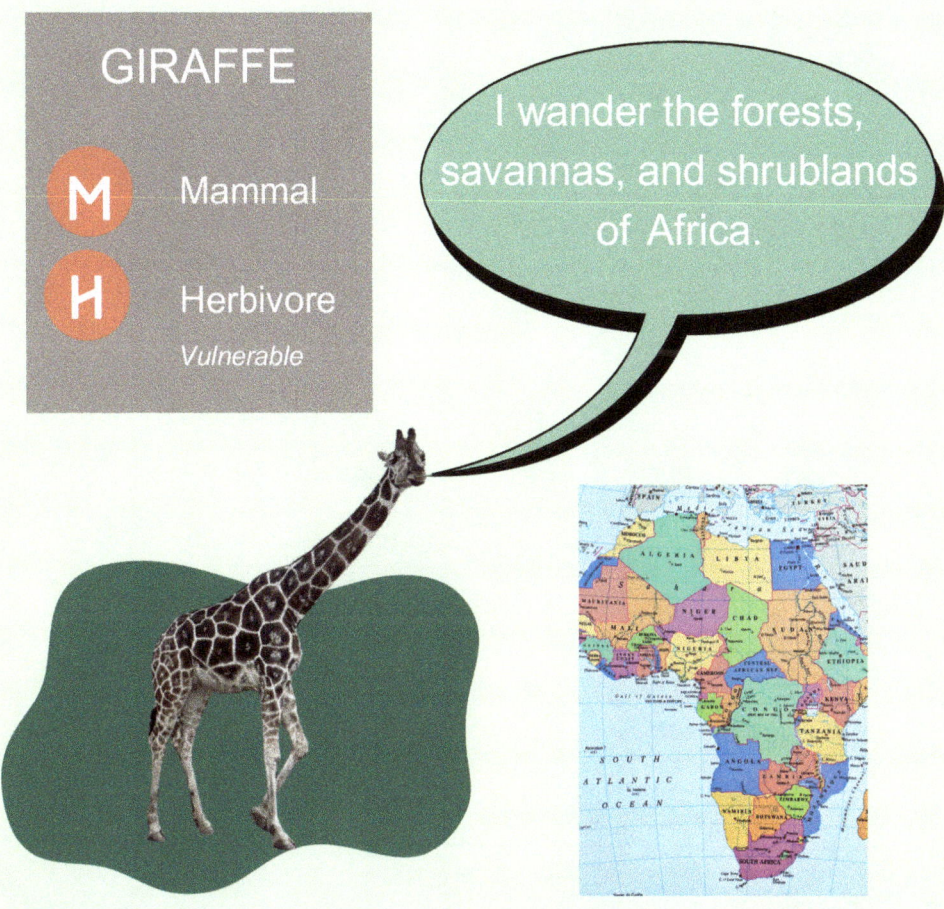

H is for
HUMBOLDT PENGUINS

H is for Humboldt Penguin. I am a bird.
Some think I'm a mammal, but that is absurd.

I lay eggs, I have feathers and wings and a beak.
A little awkward on land, but I'm not a geek.

I wear a tuxedo wherever I go.
I live in warm climates and I don't like snow.

What else can I tell you? There is so much more!
But Ifolas are waiting. They're next on the tour.

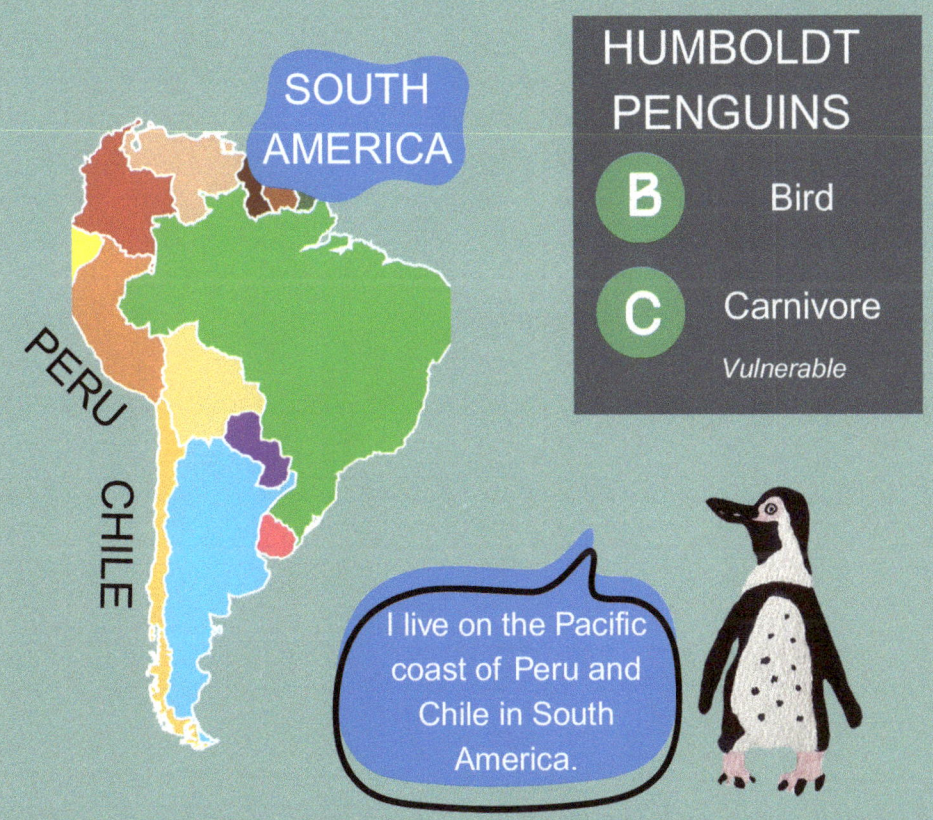

I is for
IFOLA TREE KANGAROO

I is for Ifola. I'm a tree kangaroo.
You'll find me in New Guinea or maybe a zoo.

Unlike my hopping cousins, I live in a tree
I do have a pouch, and my babies stay with me.

I'm slower than a sloth. I'm quiet and don't shout.
I'm super cute and cuddly, of that there's no doubt.

What else can I tell you? There is so much more!
Javan Rhinos are waiting. They're next on the tour.

IFOLA

M Mammal

H Herbivore

Endangered

I only live on the island of New Guinea which is close to Australia on a map.

NEW GUINEA

← IFOLA HABITAT

J is for
JAVAN RHINOCEROS

J is for Javan Rhinoceros or Rhino.
I've been around since the time of the dino!

My skin is like armor. I don't use it to fight.
Well, maybe a little against an insect bite.

I use my poop and urine to decorate,
When other rhinos smell it, we can relate!

What else can I tell you? There is so much more!
 Koalas are waiting, They're next on the tour.

JAVAN RHINOCEROS

 Mammal

 Herbivore

Critically Endangered

I can only be found in one place in the wild: Ujung Kulon National Park on the western tip of Java, Indonesia. As of 2020, there were only 68 of us.

K is for
KOALA

K is for Koala. And I am not a bear.
Born the size of a jelly bean, blind with no hair.

So I ride in a pouch on my mama's back.
Until I grow strong and face no attack.

No two alike, my fingerprint is my nose,
And I groom myself with my special fused toes.

What else can I tell you? There is so much more!
But Leopards are waiting. They're next on the tour.

"I live in Australia. Did you know Australia is a country and a continent?"

KOALA

 Mammal

 Herbivore

Vulnerable

L is for LEOPARD

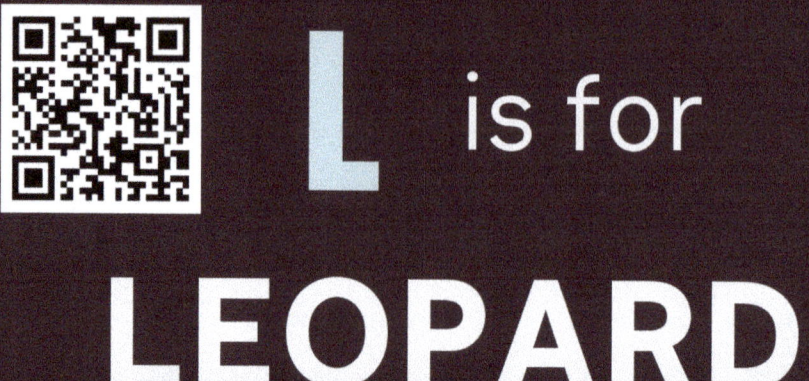

L is for Leopard, a super, skillful cat.
I can swim and hunt in water. How about that?

I can carry my prey while I climb a tree.
My nocturnal vision helps me to see.

I can jump 20 feet in a single leap.
I hunt at night, and during the day I sleep.

What else can I tell you? There is so much more!
But Mandrills are waiting. They're next on the tour.

Look for me in the forests, grasslands, and mountains on the continents of Africa and Asia.

LEOPARD

M   Mammal

C   Carnivore

Vulnerable

m is for MANDRILL

M is for Mandrill. Some think I'm pretend.
But I'm a large monkey with colors that blend.

My face is a rainbow—purple, red, and blue.
At night, my bright colors light up my butt too!

My tail's like a pom pom–just a small nub they say.
Did you know that I poop in the same place each day?

What else can I tell you? There is so much more!
But the Night Parrot is waiting. He's next on the tour.

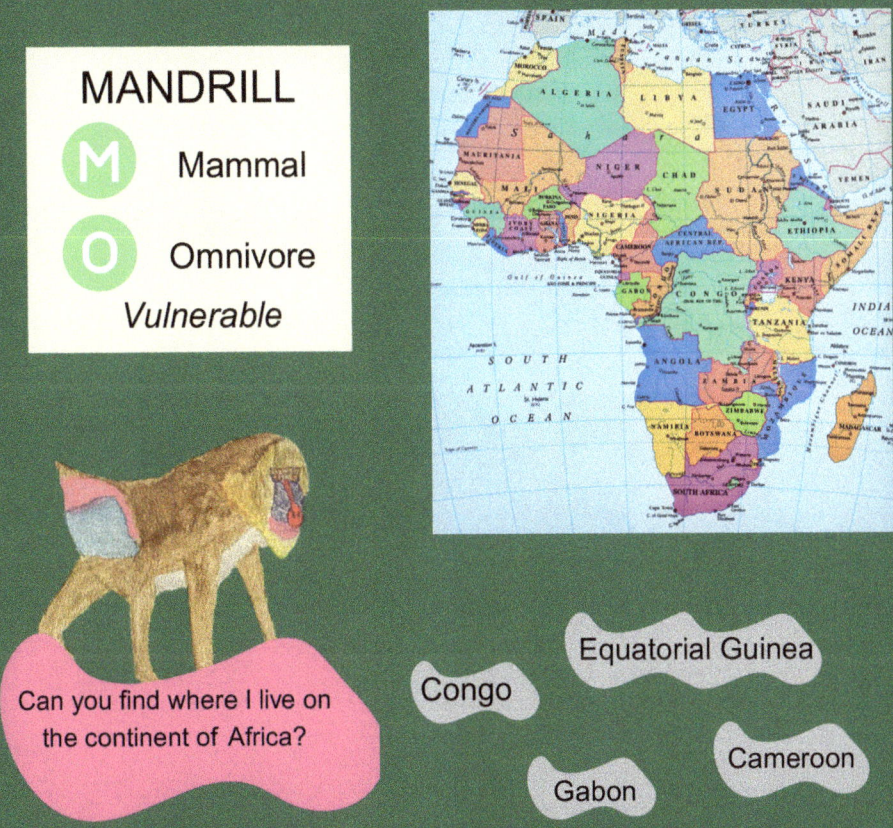

MANDRILL

M Mammal

O Omnivore

Vulnerable

Can you find where I live on the continent of Africa?

Congo

Equatorial Guinea

Gabon

Cameroon

N is for
NIGHT PARROT

N is for Night Parrot, an elusive bird.
I was once thought extinct, but that is absurd.

I'm a secretive bird, who sleeps during the day.
I'm active at night. That's nocturnal they say.

I hide in the dense grass. I don't roost in a tree.
Only parrot detectives can sometimes find me.

What else can I tell you? There is so much more!
Okapis are waiting. They're next on the tour.

I am a bird who prefers the ground to a tree!

NIGHT PARROT

- **B** Bird
- **O** Omnivore

Critically Endangered

O is for

OKAPI

O is for Okapi, a real life unicorn.
Moms are pregnant 16 months before we're born.

I have a lot of traits that make me unique.
A velvet coat with oil, that is so sleek

I look like a mix of a zebra, a horse,
And also giraffe, a relative of course.

What else can I tell you? There is so much more!
But the Polar Bears are waiting. They're next on the tour.

P is for POLAR BEAR

P is for Polar Bear, of bears I'm the king.
Largest carnivore on earth, and that's a thing!

I have a lot of blubber and very dense fur.
I'm built for the freezing cold. Do you concur?

I know that seals are cute, but that's what I eat.
Still, polar bears are cuddly. That's hard to beat.

What else can I tell you? There is so much more!
But Quokkas are waiting. They're next on this tour.

I live in the Arctic. The North Pole is in the Arctic so Santa Claus is my neighbor.

POLAR BEAR

M Mammal

C Carnivore

Vulnerable

Q is for QUOKKA

Q is for Quokka. I am cute as can be.
When I was a baby, they called me joey.

I'm a marsupial—once snug in a pouch,
With the happiest smile—no reason to grouch.

Posing for a selfie? I might just drop by,
But touching me's illegal, so let's not try.

What else can I tell you? There is so much more!
Red Pandas are waiting. They're next on the tour.

QUOKKA

 Mammal

 Herbivore

Vulnerable

R is for RED PANDA

R is for Red Panda. That's what they call me.
But I'm more like a raccoon, don't you agree?

Just look at the Superman mask that I wear.
And my tail? My tail is no tail for a bear.

I'm cuddly and cute. I can dance and I play.
Leaping and bounding through the treetops all day.

What else can I tell you? There is so much more!
Siamese Crocodiles are waiting. They're next on the tour.

S is for
SIAMESE CROCODILE

S is for a reptile, Siamese Crocodile,
My bite is vicious, but I have a great smile.

I have flaps that close my ears whenever I dive.
I can go months without eating and still thrive.

I'm an apex predator–top of the food chain.
So why am I endangered? Humans are my pain.

What else can I tell you? There is so much more!
Tasmanian Devils are waiting. They're next on the tour.

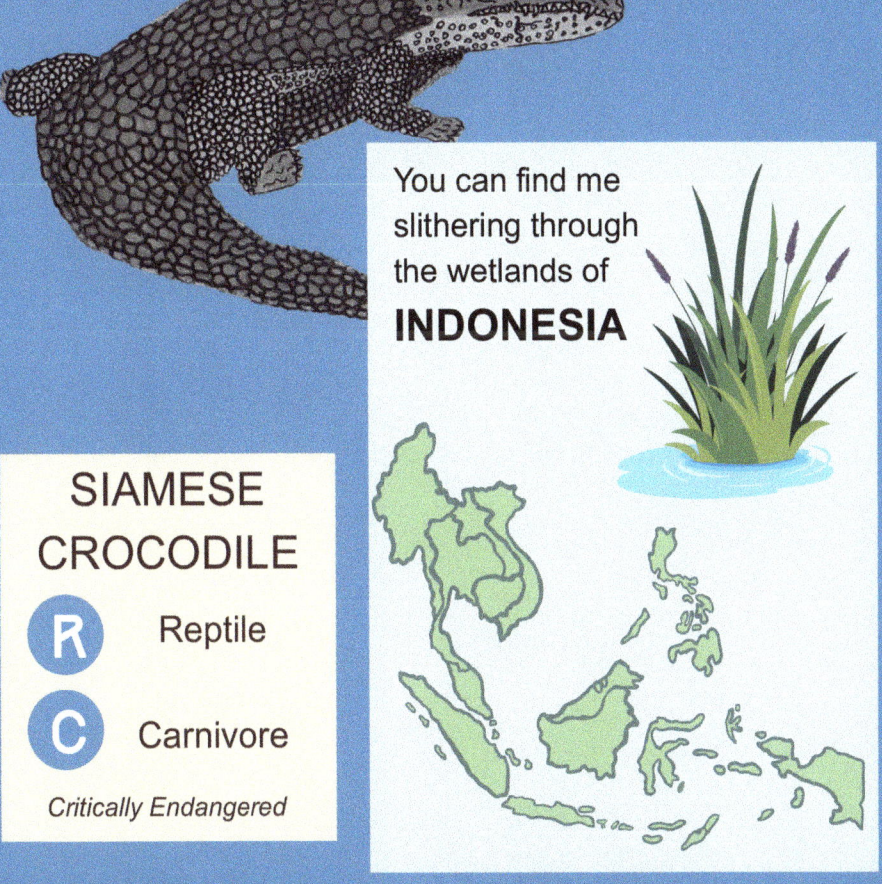

You can find me slithering through the wetlands of **INDONESIA**

SIAMESE CROCODILE

R Reptile
C Carnivore

Critically Endangered

T is for TASMANIAN DEVIL

T is for Tasmanian Devil. That's me.
I am fierce, but I'm shy and also funny.

Sometimes I get the zoomies just like you.
I run around like crazy, that's just what I do.

If you see me yawn, it does not mean I am tired.
It means, "back off," you don't want to see me wired.

What else can I tell you? There is so much more!
Utah Prairie Dogs are waiting. They're next on the tour.

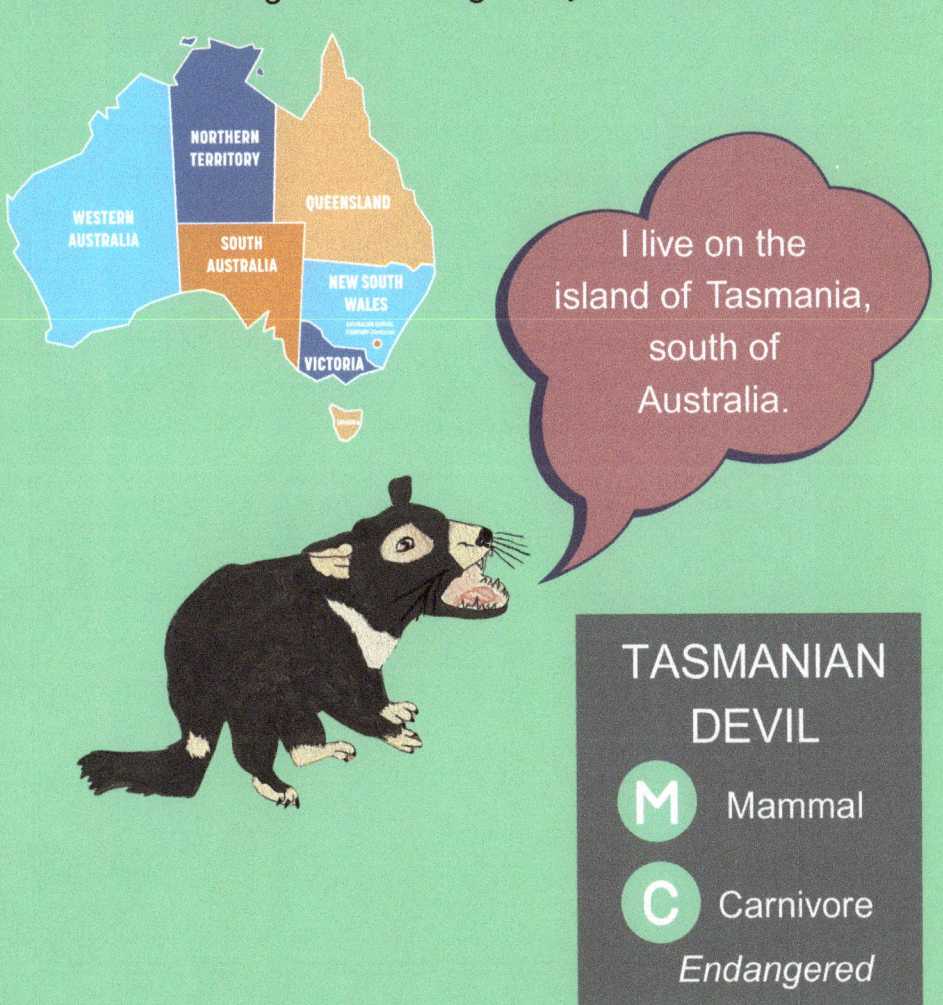

I live on the island of Tasmania, south of Australia.

TASMANIAN DEVIL

M Mammal

C Carnivore

Endangered

U is for UTAH PRAIRIE DOG

U is for the dainty, Utah Prairie Dog.
I chirp, chatter, bark...my prairie monologue.

My family and I live in towns underground,
With tunnels and apartments all safe and all sound.

I'm a social creature—I greet with a kiss,
And Utah applauds me. It's prairie dog bliss

What else can I tell you? There is so much more!
But Vaquitas are waiting. They're next on the tour.

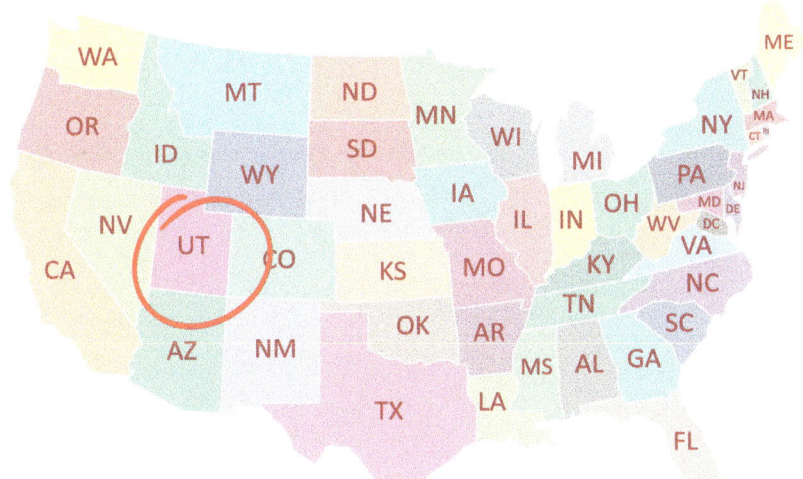

UTAH PRAIRIE DOG

M Mammal
H Herbivore
Endangered

V is for VAQUITA

V is for Vaquita. There are only ten of me.
None in zoos. I can't survive in captivity.

No one knew I existed till 1958
By then I was in danger. It was almost too late

With fancy facial features and a sweet, round nose,
My black lips are always smiling, despite my woes.

What else can I tell you? There is so much more!
Western Gorillas are waiting. They're next on the tour.

I can only be found in a small part of the Gulf of California and I hide real well.

VAQUITA

M   Mammal

C   Carnivore

Critically Endangered

W is for
WESTERN LOWLAND GORILLA

W is for Western Lowland Gorilla.
A new nest nightly, so I don't have a villa.

When I want to send a message, I beat my chest.
And walking on my knuckles is really the best.

Both my fingerprints and noseprints are unique.
Grunts and hoots and low rumbles is how I speak.

What else can I tell you? There is so much more!
Xingu River Rays are waiting. They're next on the tour.

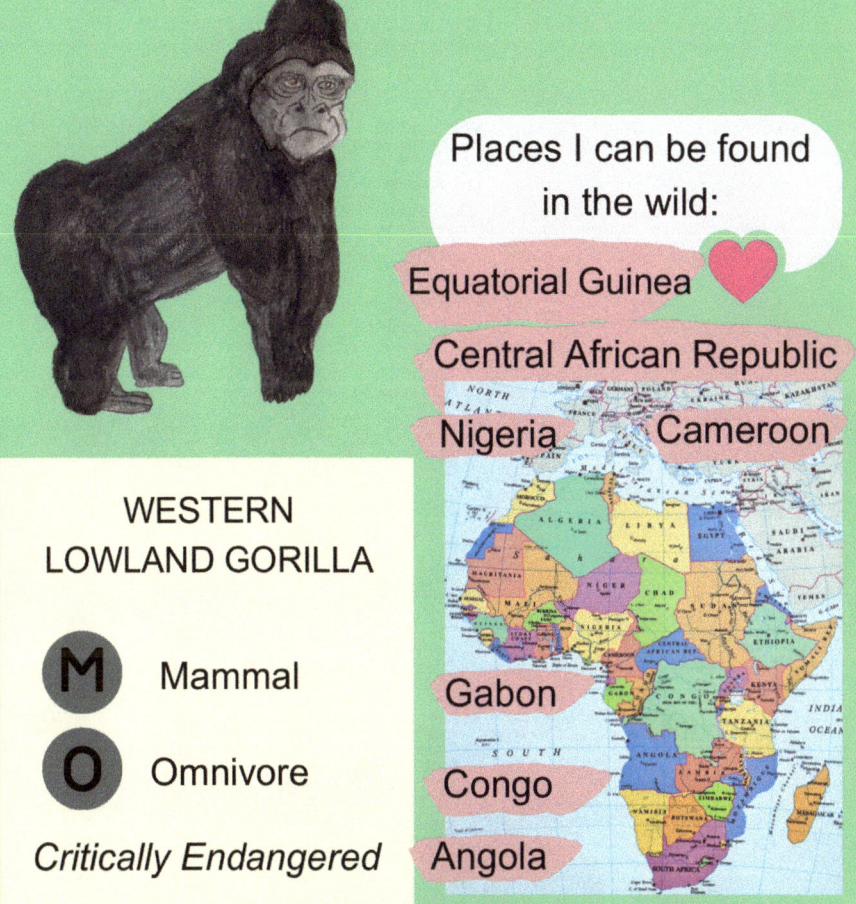

Places I can be found in the wild:
Equatorial Guinea
Central African Republic
Nigeria
Cameroon
Gabon
Congo
Angola

WESTERN LOWLAND GORILLA

M Mammal
O Omnivore

Critically Endangered

X is for XINGU RIVER RAY

X is for Xingu River Ray. I am a fish.
A freshwater stingray. My long tail goes swish.

All polka dotted, no two rays are the same.
Venomous barbs on my tail if my enemies came.

I'm as flat as a pancake, my eyes are on top
My mouth underneath and my tail helps me stop.

What else can I tell you? There is so much more!
Yunnan Box Turtles are waiting. They're next on the tour.

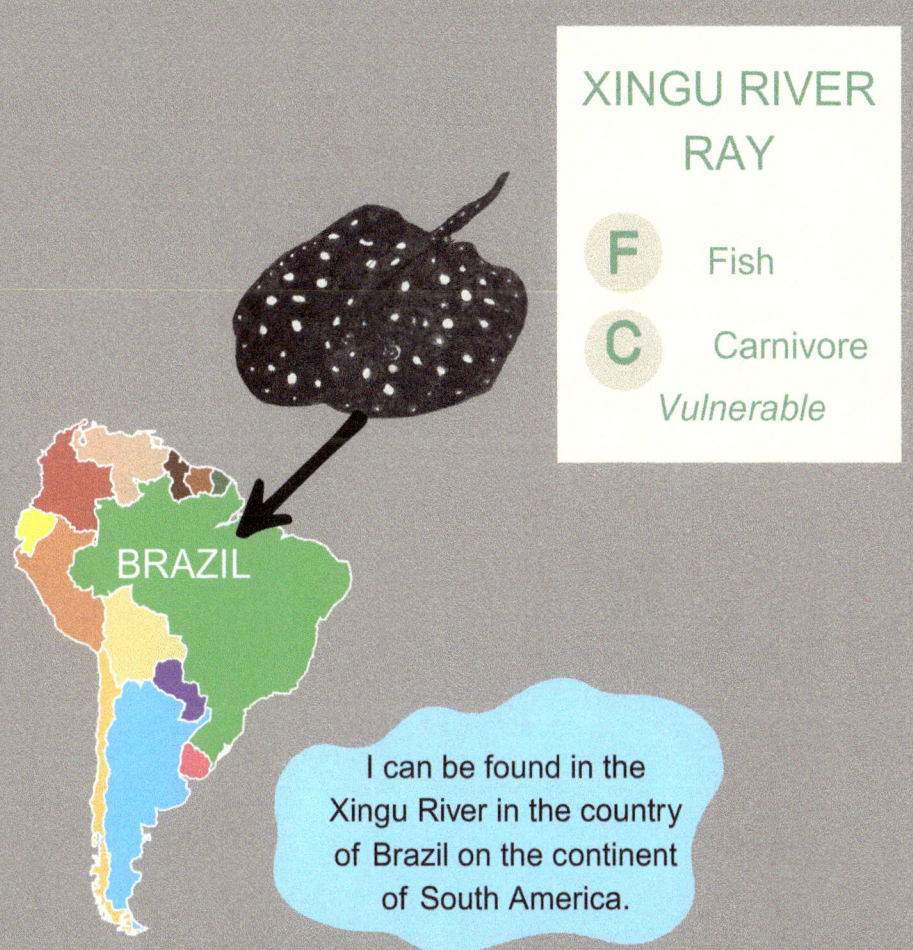

XINGU RIVER RAY

F — Fish
C — Carnivore
Vulnerable

I can be found in the Xingu River in the country of Brazil on the continent of South America.

Y is for
YUNNAN BOX TURTLE

Y is for Yunnan Turtle. I'm the box kind.
Once thought extinct, but I was just hard to find.

Did you know that my shell is made of keratin?
Guess what! So are your ears, your hair, and your skin!

Don't remove me from my home. It gives me stress.
Not just me—it's all box turtles, I confess.

What else can I tell you? There is so much more!
But the Zebras are waiting. They're next on the tour.

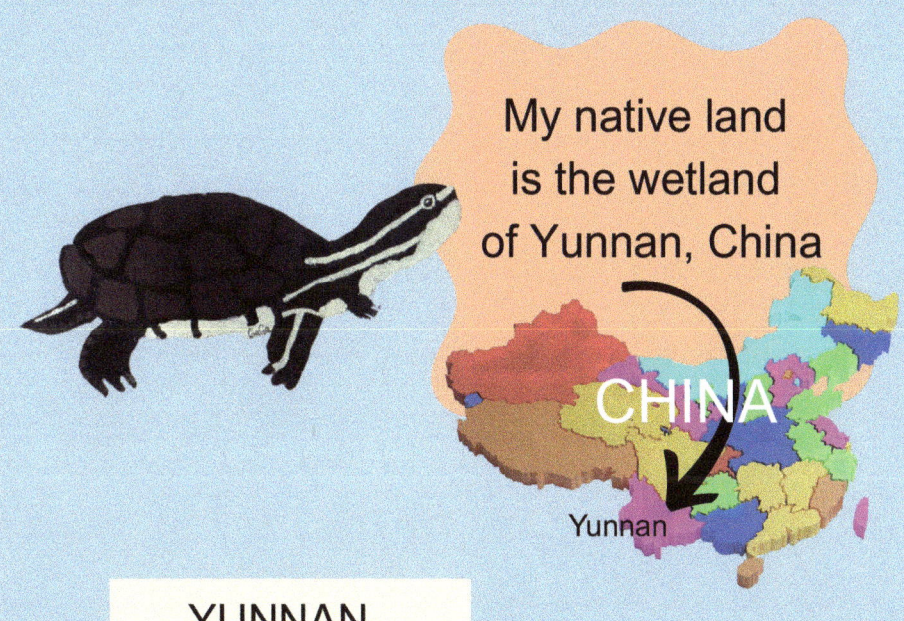

My native land is the wetland of Yunnan, China

CHINA

Yunnan

YUNNAN
BOX TURTLE

R   Reptile

O   Omnivore

Critically Endangered

Z is for
ZEBRA

Z is for zebra. There are three different kind.
Grevy, Plains, and Mountain, the types you will find.

Grevy are endangered, the other two not yet.
But if we're not careful they'll be next, I bet.

A zebra's skin is black and the stripes are white.
Although they look like horses, look out they'll bite!

What else can I tell you? There is so much more!
But I have to go now. It's the end of the tour.

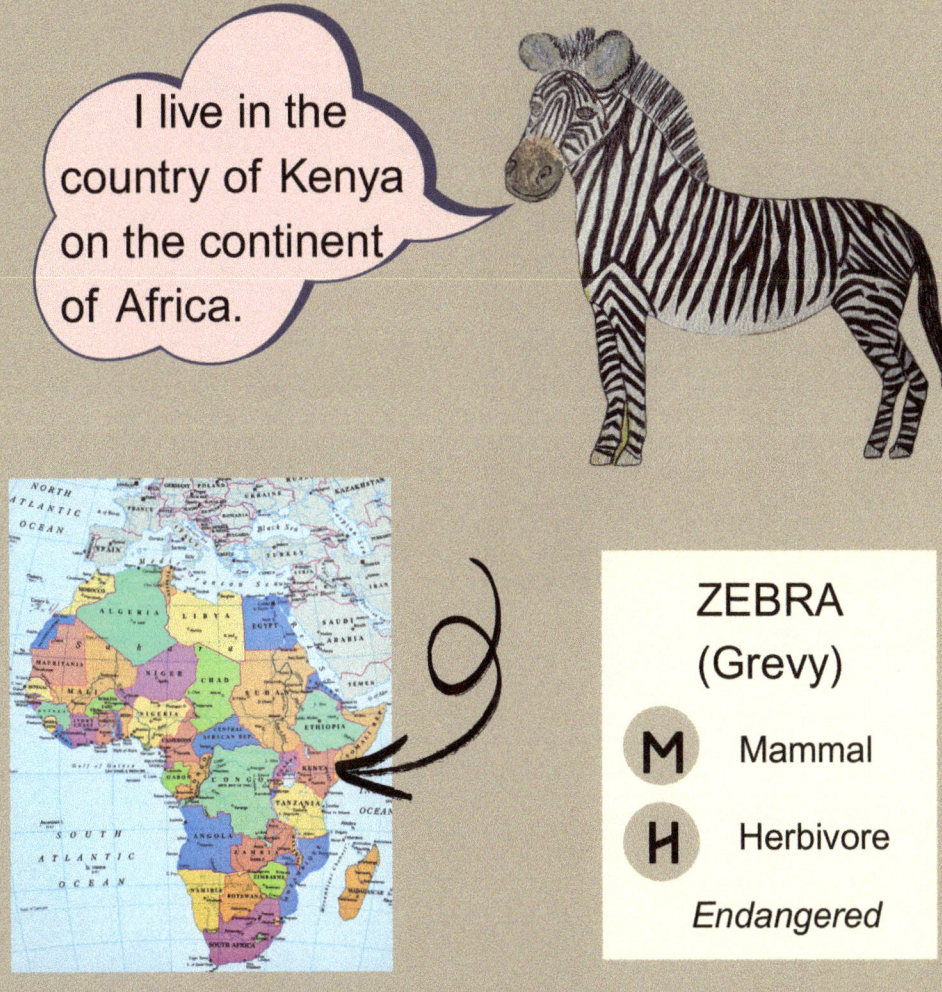

I live in the country of Kenya on the continent of Africa.

ZEBRA
(Grevy)

M — Mammal

H — Herbivore

Endangered

An endangered animal is any type of animal that is in danger of disappearing forever. If a type of animal dies out completely, it becomes extinct.

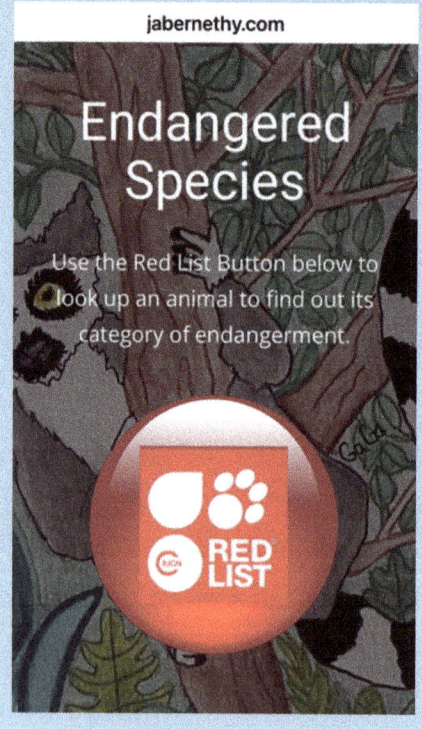

Endangered Species

The red list button takes you to the official list of Endangered Animals.

RED LIST

CATEGORIES OF THREATENED SPECIES

- EXTINCT (EX)
- EXTINCT IN THE WILD (EW)
- CRITICALLY ENDANGERED (CR)
- ENDANGERED (EN)
- VULNERABLE (VU)
- NEAR THREATENED (NT)
- LEAST CONCERN (LC)
- DATA DEFICIENT (DD)
- NOT EVALUATED (NE) or DOMESTICATED

Would you like to learn more about animals? Join GaGa's Animal Adventure Club!!!!

Scan to Join

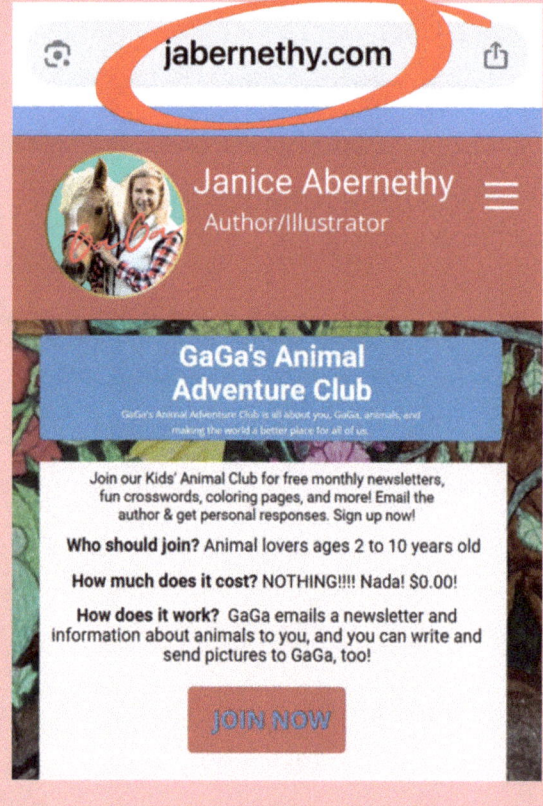

GaGa's ABC Animal Adventure Club sends monthly worksheets straight to your inbox. GaGa matches the worksheets with your age and interest. The best part--it's FREE!!!!!

About the Author

GaGa Abernethy is the whimsical pen name of Jan Abernethy—an award-winning children's author, lifelong educator, and devoted animal enthusiast. With over two decades of experience transforming her fifth-grade classroom into a vibrant living habitat, Jan inspired curiosity through hands-on science, storytelling, and play.

Today, she lives on a 60-acre ranch in Pennsylvania known as Abernethy Acres, where she and her husband Sam care for horses, dogs, cats, and one tortoise named Thurman. As a mother of three and grandmother of two, Jan continues to spark wonder through her writing, blending her deep love of animals and science into rhythmic, fact-filled stories that grow with young readers.

Jan holds a B.S. in Elementary and Special Education, as well as a Master's in Instructional Media. Through her GaGa Abernethy brand, she creates interactive books and activities that turn learning into an adventure—inviting children to explore the natural world with joy, curiosity, and imagination.

www.ingramcontent.com/pod-product-compliance
Lightning Source LLC
Chambersburg PA
CBHW052034030426
42337CB00027B/4998